CW00496246

Be

With

You

Thoughtless Reality

Be With You

Thoughtless Reality

Shri
Ramakant Maharaj

Editor Ann Shaw

©Ann Shaw
First Edition: 2016

ISBN: 978-0992875640

Published by

www.ramakantmaharaj.net
www.selfless-self.com

Preface

Be With You – Thoughtless Reality contains the direct, spontaneous teachings of Self-Realized Master, Shri Ramakant Maharaj. How fortunate we are that this Master speaks English! Now there is no question of the meaning being altered, or lost, in translation.

These precious, sacred utterances of universal import have never before been heard so clearly. They are fresh, penetrating and provocative, offering the shortest-cut to Self-Realization.

This pocket-sized book of direct hammering is designed to jolt and awaken seekers out of their illusory dream-world slumber. Page after page, drops of nectar begin dissolving your illusory concepts, reminding you of your forgotten identity by impressing Reality in you.

This book is not to be read like

other body-knowledge books that have been written only with the mind and intellect. The Master is not sharing thoughts or ideas. This knowledge is 'beyond words and worlds'. It comes from the 'bottomless bottom' of Reality. What is presented here - using the necessary medium of words to communicate meaning - is Thoughtless Reality in essence, speaking to your essence, your essential nature. One Essence, Oneness. This means Selfless Self-Knowledge that is prior to, and beyond, the body-form.

The Master tirelessly reminds you of your True Identity. "You are Ultimate Truth, Ultimate Reality. There is nothing except your Selfless Self". The Master or Guru's words are not up for debate. He is sharing Truth, your Truth, your Reality. All that is needed is your acceptance. Then, simply stand back, and witness the miraculous transformation!

"Know yourself in a real sense before it is too late, otherwise you will be shaking and trembling with fear on your death-bed", cautions the Master. *Be With You* is a clarion call for us all to awaken from this long dream called life. It is charged with a sense of urgency and immense power that effectively penetrates the layers of illusion.

"Let this Truth hammer the ego, so that you will be able to reclaim what is rightfully yours - the Missing Truth. Life is diminishing every moment, so don't take this knowledge casually. Look at you! Be with you!" urges the Master.

Concentrate on this knowledge, quietly letting it touch the bottom of your heart. Then, slowly, silently and permanently, without a doubt, Ultimate Reality will emerge.

Ann Shaw, *Editor*   *March 12 2016.*

Shri Ramakant Maharaj
is the rare living Self-Realized
Master. He was with his Master
Shri Nisargadatta Maharaj
(below) from 1962 to 1981.

The Purpose of
Spirituality
Is to
Know Yourself
In a Real Sense,
Erase Illusion
and
Dissolve All
Body-knowledge.

Your
Spontaneous Presence
is
Silent,
Invisible,
Anonymous,
Unidentified Identity.

You
Are
Already
Realized.

You Just
Do Not
Know It.

You Have Read

All the Books

But

Have You Read

The Reader?

Do Not Take My
Words Literally.

It is What
I Am Trying
To Convey
That Is
Important.

The Meaning
Behind the Words.

All That You Know is
Untruth.

That Which You Do Not
Understand,
That Which is
Beyond Knowingness,
Is Truth.

So Just Keep Quiet.

Self-Enquiry
Leads to
Self-Knowledge

and

Self-Knowledge
Leads to
Self-Realization.

You Have Forgotten
Your Identity.
Master Reminds You.

You Are Not the Body.
You Were Not the Body.
You Are Not Going
to Remain the Body.

Open Fact.

Mind is Just
The Flow of Thoughts.

It Has No Reality
Of Its Own.

Body is Just
The Food-Body.

But You Are
Omnipresent.

You Are
Ultimate Reality.

Your Files Are Corrupted.
You Need to Install
The Anti-Virus Software
of Meditation to
Delete the
Program of Illusion.

Meditation is
The Only Way to
Reboot Your Hard-Drive.

The Master Key,
The Naam Mantra Will
Open the Door to
Reality.

You Know Yourself
In the Body-Form.

This is Not
Your Identity.

You Are Suffering
from
Chronic Illusion.

The Naam Mantra
Will Cure You.

You Have To
Come Out Of This
Whole Illusory World.

You Are Told
That You Are
a Man Or a Woman.

You Accept This Illusion.

Master Says,
"You Are Almighty God".
You Do Not Accept
Your Reality.

Reality
Has Nothing
To Do With Words.

You Are Unborn.

Nothing has Happened,

Nothing is Happening,

Nothing is Going
To Happen.

Reading Books is
Not Enough.

Study is Not Enough.

Who is Reading?

Who is Studying?

Find Out!

When the Spirit
Clicked With the Body
All Body-knowledge
Started:

Impressions, Conditioning,
Pressures, Concepts,

Which You Accepted.

This Kept You Trapped
In the Illusory World.

Be Clear!

There is NO "I Am".
There is NO "You Are".

These Are
Only
W. O. R. D. S.

You Are Beyond Words
Beyond Worlds.

You Must Come Out of
This Illusory World.

Your Presence
Does Not
Need Anything.

So,
Who Wants
Peace?

Who Wants
Happiness?

This is a Dream
Which Has Come Out of
Body-Relations,

Which You Are Not,

Which You Were Not,
and
Which You Are
NEVER
Going to Be.

The Mantra
is a Useful Tool
That Hammers the Ego
and Dissolves
All Your
Illusory Concepts.

THEN
You Will Have
a Solid Foundation.

The Body is Made Up
of the Five Elements.

You Are Staying
On a Rental Basis,
Borrowing Food and Water.
You Have a License
For a Few Years.

As Soon As
You Stop Providing
Food and Water Then
You Get Thrown Out of
Your House.

Put
Spirituality Aside
For a moment!

Don't You See That
You Were Not the Body!
You Are Not the Body!
And
You Are Not Going to Remain
as the Body!

This is an Open Fact!

Self-Enquire!

Find Out
What You Are Not!

Remove All the Illusory
Layers On Your
Presence.

You were Never in Bondage.
You Are Free as a Bird.

Death is Illusion.
Birth is Illusion.

This Conviction

Has to

Appear

In You.

You Have Tremendous Power
and Strength,
But You Are
Unaware
Of Your Power

Because

You have Accepted
The Body-Form.

Prior to Beingness
You
Did Not Know
Anything,
Not Even the Word
'Knowledge'.

Everything Comes
Out of Nothing
And Dissolves
Back Into Nothing.

You Have Been
Thrown
Into the Ocean
of
This
Illusionary World.

Now You Must
Swim Out
of
This
Illusionary Ocean.

You Are
Limiting
Your Reality
By
Naming it.

Reality

Is Not
Up for Debate.

Your Hard-Drive
is
Choked.

Be As You Were
Before All Add-Ons.

Self-knowledge Means
Absorbing the Knowledge
That

"I Am Not the Body".

How
You
Were

Prior

to

Beingness

Is

Self-Realization.

You Are
Not
The Body.

You Are
The Holder
Of the Body.

The World is Projected
Out of Your
Spontaneous Presence.
Wake Up
From This Dream
Before it is Too Late.

This is a
Golden Opportunity
To Know Yourself
and
Put an End
To Suffering.

I Am Not
Speaking to You.

I Am Inviting Attention
of the
Silent Invisible Listener
in You
That is
Ultimate Truth.

You Have
Tremendous Power.

God is Your Baby.
God is a Concept.

Presence Has
To Be There First
In Order For You to Say:
'God' or 'God Exists'.

Without Your Presence
You Cannot Utter
A Single Word.

Your Presence
Is
Everywhere.

You Are
Beyond The Sky.

There Is No
Individuality.

Everything Comes Out of
Nothing and Dissolves
Back into Nothing.

And in the Nothing
There Appears
To Be Something.

When You Don't Know
Any Better
You Accept this Nothing
As Something.

You Are
The Master,

But You Are Acting
Like a Slave
of the
Mind
Ego
Intellect.

Why Keep
Travelling
When
YOU
Are
The
Destination?

You Are
Prior
To the World,

Prior
To the Universe.

You Are
Prior
To
Everything.

How You Were
Prior to Beingness,
Stay Like That.

You Were

Totally

Unknown To You.

Presence
Does Not Know
Its Own Existence.

Presence is
Without Knowledge.

It has No Experience.
No Experiencer.

No Witness.

No Awareness.

41

You Are Worried
About Death
Because You Think
You Are Somebody.

You
Are
Unborn.

Be With You.

Just Be
With the
'Just Be'.

You Are
ALREADY
Final Truth,

Without Imagination,
Without Concepts.

Body-Form-Knowledge

Must Dissolve.

This is the
Principle
Behind
Spirituality.

Break

The Vicious Circle
of
The Ghost of Fear.

And Accept that

"I Am Not Dying.

I Am Not Born".

The Questioner
Is
The Answer.

The Invisible
Questioner
Within You
Is
The Answer.

Be With You
And
Listen From The All.

Read
YOUR
Book.

Your Edition
Is Final.

The Body
May Be Suffering
but
Not You.

I Am Inviting Attention of
'That' -
How You Were
Prior
to
Body-knowledge.

Look Within!

Read
YOUR Book.

Visit
YOUR Temple.

Search
YOUR Website.

Reality is
Not Understanding.

When You
Understand Something,

It is Separate
From You.

You Are Reality.

The Body
is the

Medium
Through Which

You Can
Know Yourself.

Without the Body
There Can Be
No
Awakening.

We Are Thinking About
the Projection
Instead of
The Projector.

Stay with the
Root Cause,

The Source
from which
the projection
is projected.

The Master
Who Shows You
Ultimate Reality
Within You,
And Does Not
Simply Talk
About It,
Is a True Master.

Take a Look at Yourself
Minus the Body-form and
SEE
How you are.

The Master
is Hammering You.

At the Same Time,
The Naam Mantra
is Hammering You.

Slowly, Silently, Permanently,

All Illusory
Concepts
Will Be Erased.

The Master is Not
Giving You Anything that
Does Not
Belong to You.

He Removes the
Ash of Ignorance,
Nothing More.

The Sun is
Already Shining.

Meditation is
Only a Process.

The Invisible
Meditator
Is
Your
Final Identity.

Your House
is Overcrowded
With the
Mind
Ego
Intellect.

Evict
The Tenants!

It is a Cage, Not a House.
You Are Staying
In a Cage
Chewing a Carrot.
It May Be a Golden Cage,
a Silver, Brass,
or Iron Cage,
Whatever Comes
Your Way.
Rich People Get a
Golden Cage,
The Poor, an Iron...
... Still a Cage.

Your Presence is
NOT
Physical Presence,
NOT
Mental-Level Presence.

Presence is Spontaneous.

It has NO Shape,
NO Form.

Don't Be a Slave

of

your

Mind, Ego, Intellect.

Go Against
The Flow.

Be a Master of Reality
And Not Just a
Master of Philosophy
or Spirituality.

A Professor May Teach
By Talking about Truth,
Whereas a Master Lives It.

Entire Power,
Entire Energy,
Entire Spirit is In You.

Everything Starts With You
and Ends With You.

The Entire World is Projected
Out of Your Spontaneous,
Invisible Presence.

The Moment
Your Body Dissolves,
The Entire World Disappears.

Who is Dying?

Who is Living?

Just
Self-Enquire.

Nobody is Dying.

Nobody is Taking Birth.

Your Home is
Not
America, India or England.

Your Home
Is The
World.

Your Presence is
Like the Sky,
Beyond Limits.
You Are Everywhere.

This is
Not an Intellectual Approach,

Not a Logical
Approach,

Not an Egoistic
Approach.

All These Things
Came After
Your Presence.

Because of this
Food-body

Because of
Food-body Knowledge

You Have
Forgotten
Your Identity.

Love
and
Affection
Are the
Literal Words
of the
Body-base.

When You Came Across
With The Body,
You Created
A Big Illusionary Field –

Beingness,
Non-beingness, Awareness,
Unawareness,
Consciousness.

Be Brave!
Come Out of the Field!

Prior to Beingness
There Was Presence.

Presence is
Nameless.

Forget About
All The Words,
The Polished Words
That We Created.

This Meditation Practice is
Also an Illusion,
But
We Must Use One Thorn
To Remove
Another Thorn.

Later On,
the Whole Practice
Is Dropped.

You Are Worried
About Death
Because

You Think
You Are Somebody.

You
Are
Unborn.

There is

NO 'You'

NO 'Becoming'

And Nothing to 'Get'.

Listen To Me!

The Whole World,
Including All the Books,
All the Masters,
All Spiritual Knowledge,

Is a
Projection
of
Your Spontaneous Presence.

You Are
Concentrating
On

"I Am"

and
Ignoring

the
Concentrator.

There is Only One Source.
YOU are The Source.
There is
Only Selfless Self.

As my Master Stated:
"There is Nothing Except
Selfless Self.
No God, No Brahman,
No Atman,
No Paramatman,
No disciple,
No Master".

Nisargadatta Maharaj
Had Exceptional Power.
I am Sharing the
Same Knowledge
With
Everyone.

This is
The Right Time.

The Figure

of

God

is

Your

Reflection.

Everything

You See

After

Your Presence

Is Illusion.

Reality

is

Engraved

in the
Invisible Listener

Which
Cannot Be
Removed.

You Are Giving
Importance
to the Seen,
And
Not to the Seer.

All Gods and Goddesses
Are In You.

The Whole World Is
Your Spontaneous Projection.

To Know Yourself
In a Real Sense,
That is Knowledge.

You Are Drowning
In Ignorance,

Drowning
In a Sea of Words.

You Are Covered
in Ash.

Underneath,
The Fire
is Burning.

Master
Removes the Ash.

You May Know
Everything
About the Whole World,
But You
Do Not Know
Yourself.

Enter
Your Own Field
of Reality.

Experiences
Have Appeared
Upon Your
Spontaneous Presence.

They Will
Dissolve.

The Melting
Process is
Marching Towards
ONENESS.

There Is Nothing
Apart From
Your Selfless Self.

There Is Nowhere Else
To Go.

To Be Strong.

STOP!
With Your Inner Master.
STOP!
With Your Inner Guru.

Forget the Past!

There Is NO Past.

Past, Present and Future
Are
Concepts.

Stop Measuring Yourself
In the Body-form.
That is
the
Great Illusion.

When You Awaken
From a Dream,
The Whole Dream - World
Just Disappears.

Likewise,
This World is
Just a Dream,
A Long Dream,
Which Will
Also
Disappear.

Presence
Does Not Have
Any Sleep or Dream.

Waking and Sleep
Are Experiences
of the body only.

There is No Day,
No Night,
No Dream.

Does Sky Sleep?

The Master
Convinces You
Of Your Reality.

Then, You Must
Convince Yourself.

Convincing Leads to
Conviction:

You ARE
Ultimate Truth,
Final Truth.

Knowledge Means
Self-Knowledge.

Devotion means
the Perfection
of
This Knowledge.

Initial stage,
You Are Devotee.
Last stage,
You Are Deity.

Devotee and Deity,

Devotee and Deity,

No Separation.

Deity Knows
Through Devotee.
Deity Lies
Within the Devotee.

Naam Mantra
is a Powerful Tool
that Dissolves
Body-knowledge,
Reducing the Force of
Mind, Ego, Intellect.

It Reminds You
of Your True Name -
Reality,
Constantly Regenerating
Your Power.

Only a
Self-Realized Master
Who Knows
All
the Details,

Can Lead You
to
Ultimate Reality.

Even After Reading
Spiritual Books,
You Are Not Finding Reality.

So, Whatever You Find,
REMEMBER!
That the Finder Itself
is Ultimate Truth.

The Finder is the
Very Truth
That you are Trying
to Find Out.

The Invisible Speaker
in ME and the
Invisible Listener
in YOU are
ONE and the same.

This is
Direct Knowledge
from the
Invisible Speaker
to the
Invisible Listener.

What you SEE
Is Illusion.

THAT

Through
which
You See

Is

Reality.

The Ego itself
Is illusion because
there is no 'I' or 'you'
or 'he' or 'she'.

There is
Nothing there.

The screen is
Completely Blank.

You Are

The

Final
Destination.

There is

Nothing

Beyond.

Stop Looking
for
Happiness
or
Reality
in a

DREAM,

and

You Will Wake Up.

Don't Leave
Yourself Behind
Till the End
of your Life.

Your
Inner Master
is
Your Best Friend.

The Entire World
is your

Spontaneous
Shadow.

You Have Embraced
The Shadow
As Reality,

Therefore
There is Fear.

Where
All
Search
Ends

There You Are.

You Must Have
Complete Trust
in Yourself,
And in the Master.

Why?
Because
You Will Not Take
One Step into the
Unknown,
Uncharted Waters,
Without Trusting
The Master.

The Unknown Came
Into Existence,
And Became Known
Through the Body.

The Unknown
Came to Be Known.
The Known Will
Be
Absorbed
in the Unknown.

I am Reminding You of
Your Masterly Essence.

You Are a Master.
No Need to Look for
Blessings from Others.

Put your Hand
On Your Own Head
And Bless Yourself.
Bow to your
Selfless Self.
Everything is in You.

Seekers Read Books, and
On the Basis of
Their Reading,
They Form a Square.

Then,
They Expect Answers
From Within the Square.

Master is Not
In the Square.
He is Out of the Square.

How You Were
Prior to Beingness,
and
How You Will Be After
Beingness Disappears,
Is the Ultimate Truth.

You are
Completely Unaware of
Your Existence,

Completely Unaware
Of Your
Existence.

We Created Words
And
Gave Them Meaning.

We say 'God' is a Deity
and 'Donkey' is an Animal.
If we say Donkey means Deity,
What Happens? Nothing!
It is Simply the Words
That have Changed,

Not the Essence or Substance.

Oneness
Has No Mother,
No Father,
No Brother,
No Sister.
These are
Body Relations.

Where Was Your
Family Prior to
Beingness?

Use Discrimination!

This is NOT an Idea,
But
The Truth.

You Were
Never Born,
So,
How Can You Die?

If You Listen to
the Source
of
Your Knowledge
With Complete Trust,

There Will Be
Spontaneous Arising
of
Your Indwelling
Power.

The Master is
Giving You
Spectacles to Wear,

God's Spectacles.

EYES
to
See Through
the
Illusory World.

That There

is

Nothing,

Is Known

Without

the Help
of the Mind.

Experiences
Are Projected
From Your Presence.

When the Experiencer
and the Experiences
Dissolve

THERE YOU ARE.

You Need

Courage

to say

"Goodbye"
to this

Illusory World.

The Searcher

Who is Searching

Is

Ultimate Truth.

You Have Read
this Book
and that Book.

So Many Books!

What is Your Conclusion?

All this Reading,

WHO is it For?

Look At You!
Look At You!

Reality is Already There,
Lying Within You.

But,

You Are Not Looking.

There is

PEACE.

It is

You

Who are
Disturbing the

PEACE.

When All Thinking
Processes
Have Stopped,

There
You Are,

in the
Thoughtless
State.

Your Presence
Was There
Prior to Beingness.

It Will Be There
After Beingness.

It is There
Now
as the
Holder of the Body.

The Guru
is
Not a Person.

He is the
Impersonal,
Unmanifest
Absolute
in
Manifest Form.

You are Trying to Know
Ultimate Truth
From Within the
Body-Form.

You are Using Books
And Language, to
Find Your Reality.

You Take the Words
To Be True, The Truth.

They Are Not.

Make Sure
That the Knowledge
You Have is
Real and
Practical.

Otherwise,
You Will Be
Shaking and Trembling
With Fear
On Your Death-bed.

You are Trying

to

Grasp
This Knowledge

With the Mind.

Your Knowledge

is

Prior to Mind.

Meditation
is the
Constant Repetition
of
Your Reality,

Until it
Finally
Sinks in.

Don't Think
About the Past

Because

Your
Spontaneous Presence
is
Your Target.

In Fact,
There is
No Search.

It is
You
That is Missing.

But Now,

The Missing Truth
Has Found You!

When
Did You Start
Needing Courage
and Peace?

Only After Presence
Came Into Existence
in Body-Form.

Something Must
Be There
In the First Place
For You To Have
a Past,
Present
and Future.
There is Nothing There!

You are Formless.
Embrace your Power.

"WHO AM I ?"

is

Not in the Circle

of Imagination

or Guesswork.

Your Presence is

Spontaneous.

You Should Come Forward
With Conviction
and
Deep Feeling,

That Says:

"Yes, I Am Almighty".

We Live With
Concepts From the
Start of Beingness,
Till the
End of Beingness.

But,
There is
No Start for Selfless Self.
No End for Selfless Self.

Be Loyal to Yourself.

Respect Your
Selfless Self.

Stop The Search!

And
Concentrate on
The Searcher,
Who is
Ultimate Truth.

Without Your Presence,
You Cannot Utter
a Single Word.

You Are
Prior to
Everything.

Knowledge
Came Afterwards.

You Are Not Concentrating
On the Thinker,
Through Which
You Are Thinking.

You Are Concentrating
Only On Thinking.

In the Absence
of the Thinker,
You Cannot Think.

Your Invisible,
Anonymous,
Unidentified Presence
is
Everywhere
Just Like Sky.

You Are Subtler Than Sky
because

Sky is
Within You.

You Have
a Wrong Friendship,
a Mistaken Friendship.
You Misplaced
Your Friendship, and
Made Friends
With the Body.

You Must
Be Your Own Friend.

Your Inner Master
is Your Best Friend.

Ultimate Truth

is

Not Being Impressed In You,

Because of

Illusory Concepts

That Are Crowding You.

Anyone Can Say,

"Everything is illusion".

But,
Accepting this
As Fact,
is
A Different Story.

You Are the
Architect
of
Your Life.

Stop Running Here,
And Running There,

Because

You Do Not Know
The Runner.

Thoughtless Thought
Will Appear.

Thought is Connected
With the Body,
But
Thoughtless
Thought,
is Connected
With
Ultimate Truth.

Don't Be So Cheap

That
You Let

The World
Pocket You.

Happiness is
Inbuilt in You.

Power is
Inbuilt in You.

There is
No Power
Outside of You.

There is Nothing
Except
Selfless Self.

It is a
Great Shame,
A Calamity,
To Accept
That
Which You Are Not,
And,
To Keep On
Crying in The Dream.

You Are to Surrender.
Self-surrender
Internally.

Bow
To Your
Selfless Self.

You Are Great.

You Are Visiting
This Teacher, or That Teacher.

How Much Longer
Are You Going to
Keep Visiting Others,
When You, the Visitor,
Are Yourself
Ultimate Truth?

Visit the Visitor.

Visit Your Own Site.

All this Searching:

"Where Am I?"

When All the Time

You Are Here.

Accept
that Reality
Is Within You.

That
Masterly Essence
Is in You.

Then,
Finally,

You Will
Stop Roaming.

Every Time
You Use Words,

You Are

OTHER than
What
You Are.

The SEER
Does Not Know,
That What it Projects,
Is its Own Projection.

What the SEER Sees
Is
Invisible,
Anonymous,
Unidentified
Identity.

Your Presence
Is Needed
For You to Say ' God '.

Without Your
Presence,
There is No God.

God is your child.

Master is
God's God.

You Are Almighty.

You Are Complete
Wholly Independent.

You Are
Father
of the World.

When You
Came Into the Body,
Did You Bring a Wife
or Any Friends
With You?

Forget About the Dream!

The Big Family is
a Dream.

Your Husband, Wife?
All a Dream.

My Presence is
In Every Being

Therefore,

Who Can I Hate?

Who Can I
Struggle With?

This is Called
Spontaneous Realization.

When the Knower

and

Knowledge

Disappear,

There

You

Are,

No Form!

Spontaneous Silence
Emerges.

Spontaneous Peace.

When Everything
Merges
into Oneness,
And
is Absorbed.

The Secret
Will Open Up
To You, as
You Identify the
Unidentified
Identity,
Prior to Beingness.

WAKE UP!

You have a
Golden Opportunity.

You Must Be Driven:

"Yes, I Want to Know
Who I Am!

I Want to Know
Reality".

This is a
Long Dream,
a Long Movie.

You are
the Producer,
the Director,

and

the Star.

Know !
And Be Quiet.

Know the Reality,
And Be Quiet.

Be
Within
Selfless Self.

You Are
Already There.

You Are the Terminus.

With the Light
in Your Hand,

You Were Running
After the Dark.

Your Presence
Was There
Prior to Everything.

The Entire World,
Including
All the Deities,
Masters,
Teachers,
is the
Spontaneous Projection
Of Your
Selfless Self.

The Master Places
The Searcher
Before You.
You Are
Seeing The Searcher.

Sit Alone,
Concentrate
On This Knowledge.
This is the Tip, the Edge.

Let It Touch
The Bottom of
Your Heart.

Slowly,
Slowly,
The Body Identity
is Melting,
and
Turning Towards
Ultimate Truth,

Where There is
No Experience,
No Experiencer.

Accept the Truth

That

You Are

Absolute,

Without Uttering

a
Single Word.

You Are Everything,

And Everything
is Within You.

There is
Nothing
Except
Selfless Self.

There is Nowhere
To Go To
Beyond
the
Direct Knowledge
of
Ultimate Reality.

I Have Presented You
With the
Golden Plate
of
Reality.

There is No Need to
Go Begging, Ever Again.

You Are
The Final Destination.

You Are
Insulting
Yourself
By Ignoring
Your
Selfless Self.

Where All Ways End,
There You Are.

Now, You Can
Throw Away the Map.

Forget it!

You Have Reached
the
Last Station,
the
Ultimate Station.

I Am Trying To
Remove You
From the
Vicious Circle of Illusion.

But Again,
You Want to Jump
Back Into the Ditch.

STOP!
Stop Your Clowning Around!

173

Samadhi is Illusion
because
YOU
Are Experiencing the Samadhi,
the Silence,
Peacefulness.

At the Ultimate Stage,
There is No Peacefulness,
No Silence.
Nothing is There:
No Witness,
No Experience,
No Experiencer.

Now You Know
That
You Are
Ultimate Reality,
Final Truth.

Pay Attention
To Reality.

Don't Neglect
Reality.

Happiness

Is a

Veil

Upon

Your Presence.

All Doubts
Have to Be
Cleared Up.

It Takes a Long Time,
For the Roots of a
Spiritual Tree to Grow.

But That Tree
Can Be Cut Down
in Minutes.

I Have Planted
The Nectar Plant of Reality
in You.
Now, You Must
Take Care of It.

You Will Come
To Know the Unknown.

But, If You Don't Water and
Fertilize it . . .

It Will Die.

There is a Statue
of the Deity
Within You Already.
It Just Needs
To Be Uncovered.
The Master Gets to Work
On the Sculpture,
Hammering, Chipping Away
The Unwanted Parts,
Until at last, the Deity,
In All Its Splendour,
is Revealed.

You Are Like Sky.
There is No 'I' in Sky.
Surrender Your Attachment
To the Body.

Dissolve Any Fear.

Use the Courage
That Comes From
Knowing That
You Are Unborn.

Keep
Surrendering
the Illusory Concepts.

Keep Surrendering

the Self,

of

Selfless Self.

There is No World,
And No Word,
For the Realized.

You Are
Utterly
Absorbed
In Yourself.

Absorb the Knowledge,
and Enjoy.

There is
No Need
For Long,
Serious Faces.

This is
Happy Knowledge
I'm Sharing.

You Are Free,
So, Be Happy!

You are ONE
With Selfless Self.

You Have Merged.
ONE
With Selfless Self.

Now You Know:
My Presence is Like Sky,
And It is
In Every Being.
There Is
No Separation.

That,
Which Cannot Be Talked About
is a
Sign of Reality.

Go Deeper,

And Deeper,

Into Your

Selfless Self.

The Door
Will Open Wide.

Open,
Open, Open,

Until You See
Your Selfless Self,

In Full Light.

There,
You will See
The Principle,

The Silent,

Silent,

Invisible Listener.

Beyond That -

Nothing.

You Want to
Stay In the
Illusory World.

But,
At The Same Time,

You Want To
Know Reality.

Impossible!

Ultimate Reality
Will Not Emerge,
Until,
All Body-Knowledge
Has Been Dissolved.

When
You No Longer
Require Happiness,
You Have Reached
The Destination.

The Cave of
Knowledge is
Now
Open For You.

Take
As Much Treasure
As You Want.

How You Were
Prior to Beingness
Is Self-Realization,
Beyond Words and Worlds.

It is Called Presence,
Spirit, God, Brahman, Atman,
Ultimate Reality,
Ultimate Truth, Final Truth.

But You Are Not in Words.
You Are Nameless.

You Are
The Master.

Decide How Much Attention
to Give to Thoughts.

If You Give
Unwanted Thoughts
Attention,
There Will Be Pain.

If You Ignore Them,
No Pain.

Go Within
And
Be Within Selfless Self.

Look At You!

Try to See the Seer.

As You Try to
See the Seer,
The Seer Will
Disappear.

Enjoy the Secret
of Your Life.

What Do You Want?
Nothing.

What Do You Need?
Nothing.

Because
You Know That
Everything is In You.

Don't Fall Into the Trap
of
Worldly Attractions
That Are Everywhere.

Remember That
You Have Created These
Illusions.

Maya
is
Your Baby.

Presence Dissolves
At the Last Stage.

You Will
Not Be Aware
When
Presence
Becomes
Omnipresence.

Be Driven By One Desire:
The Fire That Is
Constantly
Burning in You.

An Intense Longing
To Go Deeper,
and Deeper.

Go Ahead!

Go Closer and Closer
to Selfless Self.

Spiritual Knowledge
is also the
Great Illusion.

It is
There
Only To Remove
The First Illusion.

Once You Know That
You Are Not the Body,

Not the Mind,

Not an Individual,

You Will Have

Conviction.

After this
Spontaneous
Conviction,

You No Longer
Need Knowledge.

Knowledge
is Illusion.

You Are
The Worshipped,
The Worshipper,
And The Worship.

Spiritual Reality
is
Now Flowing.

Keep Chewing
the Chocolate
of
Presence.

When You Meet
The Master,
You Meet Yourself.

Spirit Sees
Its Own Reflection
In the Master,
Recognizes Itself,
Responds,
and

Starts Dancing Again.

After
Spontaneous Conviction,
There Will Be
Peace
Beyond Imagination,
And
Exceptional Happiness
Without Any
Material Cause.

Be Quiet
and
Happy,
in the
FLOW
of
Inner
Contentment
and
Peace.

Spontaneous
Happiness
Is the Fragrance
of Selfless Self.

This Means That
The Knowledge,
Your Knowledge,
Is
Being
Absorbed.

Embrace
Selfless Self
And Go
DEEPER
And
DEEPER
And
DEEPER.

Be With You
Constantly.

"Whatever I have to convey in respect of spirituality is conveyed in the book *Selfless Self*."

ISBN: 9780995473454
Available from Barnes & Noble, Watkins Books London, Amazon, Flipkart etc.

SELFLESS
SELF

Ramakant Maharaj

Editor Ann Shaw

New format with no caps or bold fonts, 500 pp. The authorized and definitive book of the teachings of Sri Ramakant Maharaj.

26429231R00124

Printed in Great Brita
by Amazon